Pause, Traveler

Pause, Traveler

poems

Erin Coughlin Hollowell

Book design and layout by David Rose

Library of Congress Cataloging-in-Publication Data

Hollowell, Erin Coughlin, 1965 –
   Pause, traveler : poems / Erin Coughlin Hollowell.—1st ed.
      p. cm.
   Includes bibliographical references and index.
   Poems.
   ISBN 978-1-59709-720-8 (alk. paper)
   I. Title.
   PS3608.O49423P38 2013
   811'.6—dc23
                        2012027700

The Los Angeles County Arts Commission, the National Endowment for
the Arts, the City of Pasadena Cultural Affairs Division, the Los Angeles
Department of Cultural Affairs, Dwight Stuart Youth Fund, and Sony Pictures
Entertainment partially support Red Hen Press.

First Edition
Published by Boreal Books
an imprint of Red Hen Press, Pasadena, CA
www.borealbooks.org
www.redhen.org

Acknowledgments

Thank you to the following publications where these poems were first published: *Alaska Quarterly Review*, "Rot"; *Blue Earth Review*, "Circus World," "Corn Palace," and "Prairie Dog Town"; *Cairn Magazine*, "In Love with the Garbage Men"; *The Crab Creek Review*, "Canal Street" and "Spring"; *Fire on Her Tongue*, "Parts of Speech"; *Hobble Creek Review*, "If it rains all summer"; *Letters to the World: Poems from the Wom-po Listserv*, "Practice"; *San Pedro River Review*, "Looking"; *Terrain.org: A Journal of the Built and Natural Environment*, "Cusp"; and *Weber Studies*, "Mud Season."

for Glenn,
who said you are home,
now write.

Contents

I

New York Echo

Canal Street

Lingering over bok choy in neat formation,
bitter clean contrast of white and green,
I hide my cold hands in my coat. Breath
fractures before my lips.

Your reflection slides past mounds
of iced fish that still gasp and shudder.
Blood oranges pass your inspection,
each held for a moment to your nose.

Handing a red pepper over your shoulder,
you list aloud the ingredients for dinner.
You speak not to me, but to yourself,
or to someone else that I often feel

moving in the pause between us.
You and I travel on parallel paths,
feet down on opposite sides of the same bed.
I pay for the perfect vegetables you choose.

The old men raise their eyebrows,
but you move on toward the corner.
On a side street, a delivery truck idles,
the back door open. A young man

in a smeared apron sits on a pile
of bloodless pigs. It begins to snow.

New York Echo

No one but us
and the wind
down a long West
Village block where streets
twist oddly.
In a darkened shop window,
an empty wedding dress
made of nails. You
laughed. The bricks
were not red enough—
someone had painted
them redder. A park
surrounded by iron
staves winked dimly.
No noise but the shift
of trash in the wind.
Your laugh. October
a starved dog,
the hollow street,
your fingers
like bones.

Atlantic Avenue Idyll

I.
Stairs wind through piss-ridden
shadows, green crazed linoleum.
One hand clutches the greasy banister
as she hauls herself with groceries
up seven flights at nine p.m.

II.
Below, the surge and slack of salsa
carries through the pipes and cracks.
She eases off her sneakers, gray
and pitted from subway grime. The boy
has not even opened his bedroom door.

III.
The chime of ladle on plate brings him.
He slides into the cracked plastic chair.
Her exhausted questions, his one-word
mumbles. His back is a wall
as he washes his dish, leaving hers on the table.

IV.
The television searchlight plays on
her face as she dozes on the sofa.
Blue low flame that builds
lifetimes of infants and gravestones.
Her hands unclench in her lap.

Edge

Subway doors sever here
from there. Floors slick
with rain and gutter dirt.
Old ladies gather
their grimy coattails
as they collapse into seats.
He leans too near
the door, positioned beneath
a dented speaker that blasts
the conductor's garbled speech.

The clutched white cane
and peculiar slant of his head,
like a bird hearing a child's whistle,
are the only clues to his precipice.
Each day, he listens for the incantation,
Broadway, transfer to the A, C, and E trains,
before he rushes the door, straight
to the cold assurance of tile wall.
I watch him rearrange himself,
as the train pulls from the station,
gusts stirring gutted newsprint at his feet.

Some mornings, I stand behind him
on the F train to Manhattan. I imagine
helping him get off at the correct station
without sudden panic at the edge
of the platform, delivering him into his day.
I imagine the scent of his shampoo

as I whisper into his neat pink ear,
the gentle scratch of wool
as I grasp his elbow, place my hand
on the flat expanse of his lower back.
And then later, what he might utter
as we make love, what sounds describe
a soft country suited to the blind,
filled with easily mapped terrain,
and no dangerous edges.

Salvage on the Lower East Side

Angel, eyeless, one wing lashed on with rope.
Arch carved in flowers once white, now slate.
Bathtub with lion's feet, painted completely sky blue
and chipped with a hundred stained stars.

Through doorframes and half-demolished windows,
I follow your progress, your eyes measuring
and discarding. Practiced at the art of calculation,
you have a vision and we shape ourselves to it.

I cut off my toes to fit shoes
that match the clothing in your closet.
Now you would renovate entirely,
toss it all and start from studs.

In what warehouse will I wait to be reclaimed
among porcelain dogs painted purple by junkies,
stained glass from decommissioned churches.
Abandoned in the aisles of the maimed.

Delay

People churn through Penn Station.
Little kids clench to their mothers,
women with cheap vinyl suitcases.

A few men lounge around a phone booth.
An empty coffee cup crushed
beside bolted-together plastic chairs.

Legs stretched before me,
I listen to the blurred voices,
the scuff of feet on linoleum.

The sparkle of a candy wrapper
caught in the sigh of moving bodies.
I watch for you, random particle amongst

all the other collisions and swervings.
We loved each other once.
I arrive and disappear. You arrive, disappear,

wander even farther away. Beneath
the tick of the letters flipping each time
a new train comes into the station, I wait.

I can wait. I have been waiting.

Tricks on Hudson Street

Across the street was a magic store
complete with wands and capes and rabbits
in small cages toward the back. We stopped
on the way home from work and you let me
pet their noses. Soft. Pink. You said
rabbits are stupid but not as stupid as sheep.

Once we visited another store that sold
whips and leather masks. It was supposed
to be exciting. Instead, it felt like playing
pool on a dirty table. The men in the store
didn't make eye contact, and the women
trembled like white rabbits.

Later in the subway, I watched you watch
a girl with long hair who ran her fingers
through it and your fingers twitched
like a rabbit nose. You leaned back and closed
your eyes, the rhythm of the subway a long
conversation we were both too tired to have.

Spring

I remember a taxicab pulling up
to a crowded rainy curbside.
A man opened the door for me.

Blue as storm and April,
there was a moment when his eyes
broke open to let in my face.

If I were to guess, I might say
it was like budding. His hand
reaching out to touch my skin.

You can be taken by kindness
just the same as by anger.
A small bird needs a small branch.

Chelsea

As he thrust
through some
part of me
silent too long,
how was I to know
that he was really
pushing
the pin through another
butterfly, spreading me
flat to capture
something I hadn't
known was there.
I stared at the water stain
on the ceiling of a hotel room
while he whispered in my ear
that he loved me.

And now, when it's taken a miracle
to pull that shaft back out,
leaving behind scraps of rust
that whisper liar liar liar,
how can I explain that there
is still something left behind
like love.

II

Family Portraits

Kindergarten, 1969

Masking tape straps my left hand
to thick wool stockings
that cover stick-thin legs.
The letters twitch and gambol
over the lines, little blue roads
too small to contain the words.
Again the teacher takes the pencil
from my right hand and contorts
my fingers into a duck shape,
the bill waiting to grasp.
Practicing my name, a creek
of nineteen letters curling
like the one where I catch
slick frogs and water beetles,
and there I am again, wandering.
Facing the corner, I consider
girls who sleep in bear's beds,
the sad fate of Winkies,
a dog with a clock that ticks
inside his stomach. Stories
churn inside my head.
My bound hand curves words
against my leg, while the other,
poor cripple, does
all the heavy lifting.

Playground

You were punishment,
I thought. Your eyes
flat as nickels. Your
voice slurred. Shirts
stained with food,
hair too neatly combed.
Scrape of your foot
in the gravel.

I didn't want to hold
your hand on the empty
playground. Mom and Dad
sitting at a picnic table
watching as you hung limp
and stared at the dirt, rocks,
litter beneath the swings.
I strained for creaking flight.

The dark woods crowded
near the leaning chain-link fence.
No one else brought children
to this rusted no-place.
Only our small family,
quiet in the ruin. You,
the fractured one, held their
sight. In my child's mind,
even then, I knew there
was no competing
on that front. You were
perfectly damaged.

I sat in the middle
of the merry-go-round,
its surface canted, gritty.
You pushed head down,
slowly circling me.

Family Reunion

Women stood in the shade waving
handkerchiefs
at their bosoms,
sighing over how large
their children had grown.
In an arc
facing the muddy
horseshoe pit,
the men lounged
in folding chairs and drank
beer from aluminum cans. Breathless
summer pressed upon us, the woods
buzzing in sunlight
like flies around the outhouse.

My mother stood watch
at the giant kettles of corn
that boiled and swirled. Raw meat
glistening on paper plates,
the fat soaked through
to grimy oilcloth on folding tables.
She wouldn't let me eat
anyone else's food,
didn't trust her own family
to wash their hands.

On the back of a pickup truck,
an old man in a porkpie hat
played fiddle. Two uncles
rolled cigarette after cigarette,
tossing the butts at a half-bald dog.

My cousins yelled in the woods.
My father pushed me toward
the dapple, but I held
back. Blood is blood, he said.
Blood is blood.

Story to Improve Behavior

The littlest sister
in the family
of merciless lack
wakes every morning
to birdsong like pennies
tumbling in a glass jar.

She puts on threadbare
clothing of celebration;
night has allowed her to pass
through the collapsed
tunnel of dreams.

There is fruit
at breakfast,
a bowlful of bees,
and perhaps tea.

All afternoon she reads
about stones and lies beneath
the crabapple tree, alone.

She whispers fairytales
of silver keys
and broken locks.
After a dinner
of radishes and cream,
night comes.

At rest beneath
the moon-sprung sheets,
she hums the little music
of everything
taken away.

Mother and Daughter Watching

So we stood at the front window facing the lake
as my father threw the lines on the dock.
The boat withdrew over waves like shattered glass.
My lover crouched beside my father, his eyes away
toward wherever they were pointed. Trees bent
and the wind picked up white sparks
far out from the shore.

There is a place where conversation ends.
Where a person becomes a house with a locked door.

My mother lifted binoculars to her face. The boat was now
a driftwood speck, a mote in my eye. The lake had its own
purpose, its own cold methods. "Does he know how to swim?"
she asked, putting down the binoculars and heading back
to the kitchen. So many things waiting
to be cut up.

Drift

standing in line
blue evening bruise in her eye
dusk turned to stone
empty bowl like bone
struck with the lightning's gift
broken voice in rootless years
unstrung loom
thunderstorm nocturne
traveling bag prophecy
illusionary horizon
shoes worn at the heels
yellowed legacy newsprint
crumbling ceiling
gravity's answer

Family Portraits

This one pulled down bees in the sheets,
her bed became a brilliant flame.
Her hair rippled back from her face.
She touched his shoulder like a bird.

This one drove a man who had beaten his wife
to the bridge and goaded him to jump.
He crossed his legs and looked straight out,
his pipe dangling from one hand.

This one smelled of breast milk, maple leaves,
and the dirty fingerprints of boys.
She wore a white blouse and a borrowed
brooch, a clock-face supported by angel's wings.

This one spoke a language despised,
breathed fumes of clear liquor and despair.
His moustache hunkered above his wide lips,
his hands squat like blunt instruments.

In my chin she denies the world,
my unruly hair springs from his rage.
I lie at night in the bed of flames
looking life square in the face.

His Barn

Askew, timbers skewer gray sky.
Silent maples hold back
lake winds.

Long-dead men
carved their names
into rafters.

Something here hushes us,
our whispers, raccoons
scrambling.

Through broken boards, we glimpse
father, waiting
to tell this story again, his hands

ropy with veins and tendons,
his history, ours.
This place,

hay lift and pulleys
dangle. The rock foundation
crumbled, kicked away.

III

Covering the Distance

Looking

The buzz cranking over in her brain,
eyeliner smeared a bleak bruise,
skin like wax in the ladies' room mirror,
one lazy fly tapping against her reflection.

Out there, a man keeps stacking up
beer bottles, ranks of clanking. He waits,
gets angry. Wants to sweep and scatter
everything into brilliant breakage.

She is looking for a story. She is looking
for a savior. She is looking for a reason
to go home alone. To become more
than an empty bowl and a bare back.

He is looking for warmth. He is looking
for a reason to be better than his father.
If he could find that key, he would hang it
from the rearview mirror in his pickup truck

and drive all night away from this place.

Nowhere

Moth dust lonesome radio
hole in the ground
rusted Ford truck
long ride home

three red leaves
blue feather
mailbox on a stump
rabbit foot keychain

tin can full of rain
coil of rotted rope
splinter diamond glass
long ride home

tilted front porch
deer antler handle
one bent spoon
twilight gravel footsteps

Little Gem

The woman rearranges her cigarettes, checks her hair
in the distortion of the tabletop jukebox, flips
listlessly through threadbare songs by Elvis.

She moves the fork parallel to the bent knife, nudges
her water glass so that it reflects the streetlight
into the spoon. The waitress brings another

late night bitter cup. Slumped at the counter
before neon-blue-tinged slabs of apple pie,
two truckers mutter about snow on I-81 North.

Outside, diesel engines rumble through the dark,
heartbeat thrum of big wheels on wet road.
Inside, the windows weep.

Truck Stop, Route 81

Gas station lights stab
out shadows,
a girl behind
the counter making
her ninth
pot of coffee for the evening.
Everything
uncomplicated by time. How
can I find another way
to silence
accusations except
by the road's hum,
wheels beating irregular
but hypnotic?
Two states back
you are breaking beer bottles,
bursts of glass
moving farther off. Tract homes
and strip malls stand
between us, empty
parking lots and the final
diminishing
of long fields
of dirt scraped into patterns.
Standing in the candy aisle, twenty
kinds of sugar,
and I can't remember anymore

what I like. The girl goes outside to smoke.
I wait with the buzz of the lights,
the soft patter
of coffee falling
into a stained carafe.

Circus World Museum

Calliope windstorm.
Ghost clowns wander

the early morning, crossing
the bridge to the Hippodrome.

Elephant-colored sky shoulders
against the old barns. You walk

ahead of me, clutching
a glossy brochure to some

place that's not
here. I want to watch

two ragged ducks pass
the day on the sluggish stream.

You want to find a wagon,
a golden Cinderella, a song

made by fury and glitter.
Traveling east, traveling west,

we come to the same waypoint.

Corn Palace

Mitchell, South Dakota

The girl takes our money.
Her bright blonde hank
down her back, her cheery readiness
to answer questions.
Face unlined as if
she bathes each morning in milk
and sprinkles on freckles as after
thoughts. Four days of road
grime no meager
hotel spray can wash off.
The city far behind us
but the scent of too many
people still rank in our pores.
We want to ask what is it like to wake
each morning surrounded
by susurration of cornfields
rippling like a docile beast's
back in sun. She hands us our tickets
and motions toward the rack
of postcards. We push through
the turnstile and are gone.

Prairie Dog Town

You want me to stir these things up?
Larry in a too-tight flannel shirt plunges
his cane tip into the shuddering cage
filled with rattles like gravel on tin.
The snakes rear and strike against
the barricade. He stands back, arms crossed.

There's no room for me in your life.
I tell you in the car somewhere between
Kansas City and Denver. The long stretch
fills with miles of wheat, dust devils
flare on the road's shoulder as we pass.
Your eyes never flicker from the center line.

Don't miss the six-legged steer or the jackalope.
In the yard, shabby pygmy goats rush us,
clattering across bare dirt. A father
poses his three daughters in front
of a disheartened steer, its deformity
exposed behind the blond pigtails.

Don't you have anything to say?
Wind pushes dark, fast clouds
across high sky. Hand-painted
billboards for famous pie. Abandoned
filling stations and houses. Johnny Cash
singing about love and prison.

Reconstruction Arc

1.
Sunlight splits the air
in great hanks. Three broken chairs
and a single mattress smothered
with a torn quilt. A bottle of wine,
a cigarette perched in one hand.
My skin beneath your green gaze.

2.
The garden melts. Slimy brown stems
sink into the earth. One red spark twists
and flutters from beside a gray
rock. One impossible leaf.
My mouth tastes like apples.

3.
If I could, I would strip
to the bones and rebuild.
Hammer and nails.
Dirt and stone.

Covering the Distance

The air in your lungs has whistled through
six other people's lungs before it got to you
as you shift in your seat at the rear of the plane.

Ranks of heads nod and dip in a dance
choreographed by high pressure and clouds.
Music of wind on metal, music of hidden machines.

The reed of a child's cry bends against the ceiling.
Sunstruck, in this moment you are trapped
in belief, that church, the clouds spreading below
like a plush solid carpet, a pure cushioned expanse.

Everyone on the plane with you is at the mercy
of a shared conviction in Bernoulli's principle,
that speed coupled with air over a specific curve
will yield lift; look at birds, they do it every day.

How different is this than the trust we have waking
that this day will be different,
that today we might understand our little gods?

IV

Cusp

Cusp

Puzzle of bones, try to take time
out of a watch, stop sundown.
It's all the same weave, all warm
from the compost, erasing
the written page to blankness.

In the morning, the shadow
of a hawk split the yard.
Inside your ear, mother's voice—
stay away from that wall
or you'll fall, you'll feel, you'll see
over. There's another world inside.

In your pocket, you carry twelve black
stones, rosary of willing deceit,
accounting of misspent deeds.
If sand fills your mouth, spit. If salt
burns like a flame inside you,
ignite. Any shard can split
open your precious whole.

There is a crust, a crypt, a bomb
crouched inside. You witnessed blue
fragments of birds stabbed crimson
by black beak. Maybe it is blood.
Maybe it is only berries, too
ripe. *Everything tumbles.*

The Lesson

A spade can cleave
an unseen rock
if it strikes the perfect place.

My heart,
a glass fist,
ornamental, mute.

This world cultivates
sudden roots.
Not to watch
is to stumble.

Cold mornings before sunrise,
the late winter sky, tin
punctured
by stars.

I open the box of new day
to discover
a blessing,
hours enough
for a thousand mistakes.

All around the world,
a cry is passed.
In agony or triumph,
the sound rings the same.

Metal against stone beneath soil.

Mud Season

Heads bent all morning over the bucket,
we added water from the rain barrel and
stirred with a stick until the mud swirled
smooth and slick. Two small grimy hedge
witches, we crouched inhaling the dark tang
of decay, and painted the grass and marked
our faces with the carefully mixed concoction.
If hours passed, we did not notice for we sank
besmirched and enchanted in glistening mire.

Now March mud inspires a frown, a brush
from cuff and shoe. I scowl at the dog for
rousting about the yard and roiling up the
grass. No longer malleable, I see through
a narrow slot, separate the world into this good
and that bad. Yet this false spring,
breath of soil released, this churning underfoot,
is enough to unhinge me from the ice.

Fortune Teller

Spreading out her deck of rain,
cards snick to the table.
She shakes her hair—winter
silence. A different game
by the small fire.

White stones and black on the walnut
board, patterns. All the long dark months
we tried to read them, find her method
instead of the baffle of her incessant
humming.

What did we expect? Integrity
is a reticent thing. We wanted to
go through her pockets come spring,
spill out the beads and seeds, find
proof.

All summer she shared her coins
until we forgot. The tree line ripe
with whispers. She taught you a snare
with string, and for me, a way to win
at anything.

Tashlikh*

for Phoebe

Down to the small green pond
that reflects like a stolen teaspoon
the underside of the world's tongue,
I brought my pocketful of stones.

I meant to cast them into the water
for you, ransoming our sins shared
across decades and different lives.
I meant to borrow your faith.

The water shivered, full of fish,
slivers of rain's dart and dance.
Leaves shifted along the edges,
training to be dirt come springtime.

What would we be without our wrongs?
The grit-stained brick of the city
and the moonlight of a mussel shell
all bound together inside our mutual story.

This sacred art of gleaning, beauty
from trash, each pebble righteous
and revered, we are the glory of them all.
My dark pocket transfigured to a shrine.

---

* Tashlikh (Hebrew: תשליך, meaning "casting off") is a long-standing
Jewish practice performed on the afternoon of Rosh Hashanah, the
Jewish New Year. The previous year's sins are symbolically "cast off"
by throwing pieces of bread, or a similar food item, into a large,
natural body of flowing water (such as a river, lake, sea, or ocean).

If it rains all summer

Cold drops
on plants crouching
over wet soil,
continual rumble
on the metal roof,
an engine running
fitfully and then regular,
rust creeping up car frames,
slime on clapboards
and dumpsters,
the scent of rot
rubbing the corners.

Finally you understand
Noah's wife in the deep ark,
animals cranky
and the children wild
with boredom, you
understand the way
she stared in the mirror
wishing herself
deep into the darkness
of her own pupils,
wanting someplace
alone,

how she must have tried
to pretend she was some
place quiet,
with sun on a white quilt
spread on the dry grass,
a book open.

If it rains.

In Love with the Garbage Men

Wednesday morning comes
with its early blue corners
and the smell of hot cotton
under the steam iron. Restless,
the garbage men prowl their
half-lit houses, not wanting to crease
their fresh shirts while the coffee drips.

They have named their trucks that gleam
as the streetlights go out and the sun
just brushes the tops of the tree-lined
streets. Dogs grumble sleepy greetings.
Everyone else sprawls mute in their beds.
Even alarm clocks on the bedside tables
hold their tongues a little longer.

The strong and silent type, garbage
men cross through the town, taking
the things we have no use for, giving
us all a clean slate. There's something
tender in the way they put the lids
back on, placing the cans in neat
ranks beside the shadowy driveways.

Priests of the ephemeral, they forgive
our excesses, remove broken toys,
shattered wine glasses, and
the pictures of lovers who left us.
They absolve us with the hushed clank
and rumble of tires moving down
the now gently awakening street.

Devotional

Everywhere today.
As I pass the newspaper
folded on the kitchen table.

Stolen Gods Recovered.

Coffee brews
while I wipe the counter.
Cracked coffee cup.
A hummingbird
whirs to the feeder
and for a moment
is still green glass,
venerable.

Dry Gods Sale.

Laundry warm
from the dryer
piled on the bed.
Outside laughter
scatters through leaves,
a girl and her mother
riding bikes. Sun
all morning long.

Offer God until September 3rd.

The garden
fractures into color.
Lupines. Bleeding hearts.
One last poppy
drops petals,
scattering scarlet.
I pull weeds with deep
roots.

The Week of Coprinus Comatus

Fragrant ghosts of mushrooms
with their fragile white fins of flesh
rise along the edges of trails
and slow roadsides after weeds die back.

Mushrooms, like memory, forgotten
in the hum of summer, reappear
shining in the dark mornings.
A wet wind pulls at the last leaves.

The soft underside of such mushrooms
lies tender on the tongue, mingling of earth
and rain. Tomorrow they'll have dissolved
into the ink of their splendid fruition.

Walking the mushroom path, you
dwell in a different light. You remember
your brother's funeral. Your body
pulled toward the music, dissipation.

The Sounds of Things Falling

Glass sounds like sky splitting.
Pinecone like bough shrug.
Soldiers, burning ships.
Fortune like forgotten mountain.
Tears like book closing.
Head like rotten fruit.
Leaf, sweep of second hand.
Stone, door closing.
Father like mineshaft collapsing.
Tree, broken bone.
Spade like horse cart.
Façade, winter rain.
Sweat like sea morsel.
Violin like keen betrayal.
Shadow, smoke whisper.
Angel, whiteness withering.
Penny like barefoot memory.
Night, bird wing.

Practice

The morning that I dedicate myself
to looking at the world more closely,
I wake to find everything covered by fog.

The nearest cherry tree still holds
hard fists of green fruit. Its neighbor,
five feet farther away turns in tatters.

Spruce trees become towering shadows,
brooding on a vague gray horizon
only twenty paces beyond the back door.

Somewhere a dog lifts his voice
to solitary song, anonymous,
reduced to long, lone vowels.

In the kitchen, the coffee rattles and hisses
before the empty white cup. The plate
awaits the toast.

V

Pause, Traveler

Sandhill Cranes

Their voices fold back time
in gray early morning
late September. Cresting low
over the bench,
night-tinged wings
drag ungainly legs
behind them. Awakened
by hoarse calls, I rush
outside in my bathrobe.
Rain for the first
time in twenty days
stops. Spruces
drip and shudder. Cottonwoods
drop yellow tongues into puddles.
Still the cranes pass, hundreds
calling out to the mountain, to my bones,
to stars that linger in my blood.

Early Frost

Snowflakes sift out of sky like ash,
moving on the icelight breath of early afternoon.
The garden's bleak statuary of shattered stems,
crumpled handfuls of leaves frozen to soil.
Standing on the front porch, you stare at the woodpile,
willing it taller, wider—bulwark against the rattle
of elderberry branches and stripped alders.
Each winter comes a little earlier, seasons lapping
each other with the compression of years.
You wonder how long before the stream
is silenced, how long before the wind shifts.
The mountain once more wears its shroud of snow.
Stone everywhere gathers the sky into itself.

Way of a Wave

Gusts rattle loose windowpanes,
wind hurling volleys of hard rain.
The dark sea strikes all day.

Livid buzz of the coast guard helicopter
careens overhead firing every nerve
of the women whose houses face the sea.

The fleet now pent in the harbor, boats strain
against spring lines. Nets in dark heaps
on the slick dock, static squeal of radios.

Men in slickers stand on street corners whispering,
a blackened boat adrift, a survival suit washed up
empty on a beach, an October storm in August.

House on Railroad Row, garden battered
into the earth by squall. A little girl colors
at the kitchen table. Her mother stands watching.

The Way We Do It Here

First Street stretched with wind-draggled holiday lights.
The hardware store crammed with bolts and dishes,
socks, candy canes, power tools, marine paint.
Women gossip in front of the grocer;
little kids with snow boots crouch
to look at a seagull feather frozen
into a puddle. Down the block where the lights
run out, a woman puts on lipstick,
watching herself through ranks of mostly empty
bottles behind the bar. She is wondering why
her son told his teacher that she is dead.
Wondering if she will remain in the dim bar
or go home and make his dinner.
And somewhere, there is a boy falling
in love with the idea
of cutting himself, shooting
bottles in the quarry, riding
his bike down to the harbor
between the sleeping
boats into the calm,
dark water.

Wolf Moon

Towing the mountains, the moon,
a bright wheel
worthy of shopworn worship, reeled.

Town clacked quietly behind us as we rolled
farther into the outskirts,
leaving laughter,
leaving disappointment.

You checked
the mirror, watching
for a shadow, some wolf

story told at the bar. Behind us
the road kept disappearing.
Before us, snow shifted in strands over icy blacktop.

I wanted to turn around, head back, but you
would have your prize, the sight to burn
into your long legend. The massed shoulders

and star-pricked eyes. Shaggy head dipping
once, twice to your presence, recognizing
a sister in ill-used infamy. Our wheels
slid to a stop before a snow bank. Did you

imagine we might find
dark tufts of proof
on the shoulder's edge?

Meditation on the Old Year

Infinite bride of witness
sung to sleep by the whisper
of heat rising from metal,
the woodstove's mammoth sigh.

It was a war-torn year. We ate,
all of us, from the plates of sadness,
whether we knew it or not.
Now slumped before the fire,

our collective memory, pale
and fine, shrugs off its care.
Like a child with a poignant
thumb, it comforts itself,

wrapping hope like a blanket
against the bitter dark. See,
another sheaf of months,
more grids to fill in with care,

numbers adding up to a slippery
lesson. Imagine our earth
closing up over blood, growing
grass on graves unmourned.

Let us for one night
be new again, have before us
the white bird whole.

January Shallows

The duck and his mate swim circuits,
ornate hands around a blank dial.
Slough rough and dark, tides rise and fall.

Relentless, they wind the clock of winter.
He is a flash of teal and russet, a daubed dabble,
she with white patches among dusk.

Where were you when I stood watching,
ears ringing with the emptiness wind
makes when it is blowing someplace else?

I would have swum circles around your shrugs,
never aspiring to spume and spray,
a shadow always to your spark, your harlequin.

Now, I can not pretend to be drab stone,
the ledge you shelter on, the one to lift you
out of the cold and always shifting sea.

Along the shore, bare alders rankle.
The wingbeat of my heart shallows
over the shattered slate water.

Iceworm Festival

Just when the season's dark clings to us
like an uncle who's drunk too much beer,
we rake up a celebration to anything.
Iceworms, heck, why not? Throw in
a dart tournament/barbecue cook-off
and a community talent show complete
with the crowning of Miss Iceworm.

First, the Girl Scouts spread across
the stage and lisp about sisterhood.
The littlest twists her skirt in a knot.
Then local boys with their electric guitars.
Next, some women singing
in fifteen-part harmony of sorts,
a few jokes, several slightly unkind
references to the mayor. Meanwhile,
bleachers and folding chairs press
into our soft places.

When the "Citizen of the Year" lurches
up to claim his prize, swaying from damage
caused by a brain tumor, his eyes glitter
into the lights. He speaks of gratitude.
The woman behind us begins to weep,
her chair squeaking rhythmically.

Thank goodness for the coast guard boys
here to escort in five shiny girls
who chew gum and wear white sashes.
Wearing a tiara might be like wishing
on the stars stretched high above us.
Something to make night more bearable.

Roe on Kelp

She offers a piece of kelp
encrusted with herring spawn,
the small white eggs bursting
between my molars crunch and squeak.

It's important to only boil
until the kelp turns bright green,
and then lift with a slotted spoon.
You can melt butter
or pour soy sauce.

Be sure to get all you want
when the dish comes around
because there are seldom seconds.

Sometimes she pickles it in jars
so that a year passes
with this reminder of spring.

Watch for sea lions
herding the sliver fish into shallows.

Watch for ravens flying
all in one direction scraping
the sky with their voices.

It's a doorway,
it's a secret,
it's a lesson,
like where to find loganberries
or how to dry fish in a rainforest.

Pause, Traveler

Some evenings
come suddenly with the hush
of unasked-for embrace. Small lights
blear weakly on the houses, artificial
stars for this season of long darkness.
No one dares travel down the road
between the tombs of heaped snow.
Ice crazes the surface of windows.
The earth shifts.

Everything is cracked. Nothing is perfect.
Let it suffice that there is some green
gathered from the forest, some remembrance
we meant to live forever
in this long season of silence.
If we knew how the story ended,
how could we keep living it?

Rot

Carcasses blanch at the edge
of the bramble-bound stream.
Even the bears aren't interested.

The smell slips in through gaps
where wood pulls away from glass,
where wind has peeled the paint.

She doesn't eat so much anymore,
just saltines and maybe some salmon,
and tea, weak, with no sugar or milk.

In the white cupboard, behind the kitchen
where rubber boots used to pile up,
there is a river of jars, gleam of fish scales.

Her arms are scratched, picking salmonberries
along the side of the house where the garden
once grew rhubarb and maybe radishes.

Those berries, they don't taste like much,
but it hurts her to let them go to waste.

Ordinary Morning

The moon rose swollen up
like the belly of a rotten humpy.
Nancy watched it from the pump
at the only gas station in town.
Her hands shoved deep into the pockets
of the wool coat she purchased
last year at the Salvation Army.

Christ, how did gas get so dear?
Fifty bucks won't even fill
the tank. Ain't that a joke?

She sucked her teeth a bit
and wondered at the sky.
The snow sifted down
the mountainsides just fading
pink, sun set down over the Sound.
Watching the lights of fishing
boats sputter like candles in the harbor,
here she was again,
broke, cold coin
of moon deep in her pocket.

I didn't have one good haul
all summer, but my,
the water was glass
and days like a green song.

Boreal Reveal

You cannot know the night
when you'll be walking the dogs,
boots shattering the snow
as you watch the ground
for slick places that might
carry you away from yourself,
while above, all unnoticed
the light gathers together
writhing for your pleasure
and you look for the source
of the hiss that begins to sift
through the trees, and there
across the dark stage of the sky
is the eternal waltz revealed.
Oh the swirl of mysterious skirts
catches your breath
and you
fall.

Parts of Speech

The cloud speaks all in sibilance
to the moon. To the mountain,

it clanks together consonants
like old cowbells. All day

I have tried to hold still
long enough to listen.

There is a story
in the way my skin unfurls

when I've locked away industry.
It has some of the same words

that the cloud has, but without
direction—I've discarded verbs.

Alder columbine stone moss.
Fingertip thigh nape lip.

Coupled

Our courtship through letters, late in life, could never
have prepared us for the variability of opinions,
the arc of silence in a day, the many ways to disagree
without words during a long and rainy autumn afternoon.

A flock of pine siskins loops through the front yard, around
the corner of the house, and, for reasons inexplicable,
swerves into the living room's big window.
Their bodies like gravel flung against the pane.

The smell of your sleep winds its way into my dreams,
we are on a boat and the water's rough, but you hold
the wheel in one hand and a compass in the other. The chart
flutters in my arms, trying to catch the gusting wind.

Small dark birds rustle in the grass at the foot of the house,
a convulsion of feathers, tiny voices like chips of a glass
bell. At one bright rush, they are again aloft,
a synchronous movement, a marriage of meaning.

Biographical Note

Erin Coughlin Hollowell is a poet and writer who lives at the end of the road in Alaska. Prior to landing in Alaska, she lived on both coasts, in big cities and small towns, pursuing many different professions from tapestry weaving to arts administration. She earned her MFA from the Rainier Writing Workshop at Pacific Lutheran University in 2009. Currently, she is an adjunct professor for the University of Alaska. Her work has most recently been published in *Alaska Quarterly Review*, *Weber Studies*, *Terrain: A Journal of the Built and Natural Environment*, and *Sugar House Review*.

Printed in the USA
CPSIA information can be obtained
at www.ICGtesting.com
JSHW080005150824
68134JS00021B/2294